Guns and Grammar
- A book of poetry

Jennifer Rooke

Guns and Grammar - A book of poetry ©
2022 Jennifer Rooke

All rights reserved.

No part of this publication may be
reproduced, stored in a retrieval system, or
transmitted, in any form or by any means,
electronic, mechanical, photocopying,
recording or otherwise, without the prior
written permission of the presenters.

Jennifer Rooke asserts the moral right to be
identified as author of this work.

Presentation by *BookLeaf Publishing*

Web: www.bookleafpub.com

E-mail: info@bookleafpub.com

ISBN: 9789357616003

First edition 2022

To my father. Thank you for the gifts of writing and hunting. They make me a better person.

ACKNOWLEDGEMENTS

Thank you to my wonderful partner, Tony. Your love and faith have given me the courage to actually do this. Thank you for reminding me of what a badass I really am. I'm so blessed to have you in my life.

 To my boys, you are the reason my life is so full of love and laughter. You are also the reason it is so crazy, but I love you always. Remember that having a weird mom builds character.

PREFACE

My grandmother loved literature. A love she passed on to my father and to me. Some of my prized possessions are books that she gave me. She was especially enamoured with poetry. She gave me my first poetry book. The use of language and imagery beguiled her. It was something she hoped to pass on, and did she ever. I have been writing poetry for as long as I can remember. It is one of my favourite forms of literature.

My father taught me to hunt. Something my grandmother also taught him. Spending time in the bush has become, not only a way of life but also a means of self-care. Those quiet times when all you can do is watch and reflect on your life, maybe even all life, have become some of the most eye-opening experiences.

Without those two things, I'm not sure where I would be. Like everyone else, I have experienced my share of trauma, with a little t and a big T. Writing and hunting were two of the things that helped me process, heal, and move forward to a much better place in my life.

This collection is an opportunity for me to share my pains and passions with anyone who will listen. Thanks for listening.

Seasons

A snow covering
on the house top and driveway
glistens in the sun.

A crocus pushing
Up through the warming topsoil
To bloom in the rain.

An endless heatwave
Sweltering in the backyard
Thunderstorm brewing.

A heart is crushed
like a fallen autumn leaf
under my foot.

Escape

A blur of colour races past
Running, outrunning.
Feet thumping on the pavement
Rushing, racing
Air bursting in the lungs
Panting, puffing
Screams piercing the brain
Bursting, betraying

It's still there

Marching forward
Never changing

You can't escape

No matter how far or fast you run

It's still there
Always.

Resilience

You packed your stuff
You walked away
Things you promised not to do
On our wedding day

Ever emotion screamed
How much I hated you
My pride not accepting
The blame was mine, too

I see you in a little boy
That's become a better man
He has healed
from someone who ran

I am tough, I am strong
And I recover
As time went one
I found the right lover

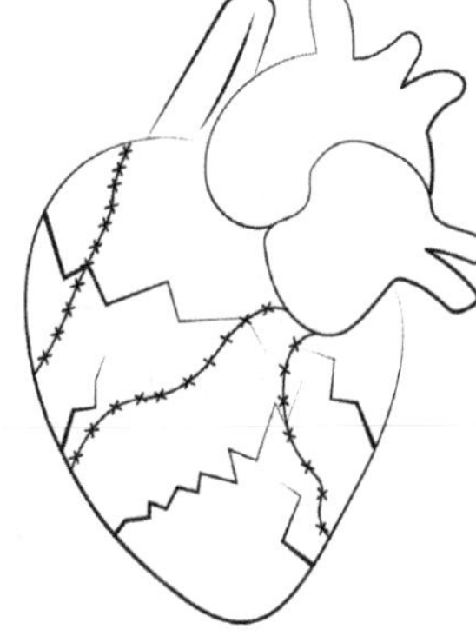

Holes

As humans,
We dig holes.
Physical holes, metaphorical holes
We dig
We keep digging

We dig for the answers
We dig for the truth
We dig up dirt
We dig up old memories
We dig at people
All this digging leaves holes

We have holes in our hearts
Holes in our memories
Holes in our lives
We have so many holes
We resemble Swiss cheese

But do these holes
Make us less?
Do they take away
from who we are?
Or is having all these holes
What makes us whole?

Broken

Your vase is broken
 You meticulously put it
Back together
With hope and Krazy glue
It works, but it never
Looks the same.
Does it need to?

Your chair is broken
You methodically put it
Back together
With wood glue and nails
It works, and it is
Stronger than before
Is that possible?

Your spirit is broken
You painstakingly put it
Back together
Glue and nails won't
Work here
At all
Is it permanent?

Only death is permanent
Lovingly put yourself
Back together

Things don't have to look
The same to still work
Can actually make you stronger.
Can you be your own glue and nails?

Power

You are strong
because
Your spirit was only bent
But not broken.
You were beat down
And you fought through pain.
Even though he tried to kill you
You survived.

Now read that backwards!

I Am

I am a river
Majestic and tranquil,
But with
The strength to move mountains

I am an orchid
Fragrant and alluring,
But with
The knowledge to avoid the coming storm

I am a tern,
Petite and fragile,
But with
The heart to journey thousands of miles

I am a cello
Deep and stirring,
But with
The power to be an orchestra

I am a poem
Thoughtful and reflective,
But with
The passion to be beautiful

I am a woman

Dreams of a Dolphin

I wish I could feel the sand between my toes,
Feel the sun on my face,
Feel wisps of hair in the gentle breeze.
I wish I could hear the bird's song,
Hear the laughter of nervous teens,
Hear the cries of forlorn.
I wish I could see the crashing waves from the shore,
See the flowers bud and bloom,
See the look of love in another's eyes.
I wish I could taste the sweetness of honey,
Taste the bitterness of lemons,
Taste the wetness of spring raindrops on my tongue.
I wish I could smell the fragrant apple blossoms,
Smell the freshly baked bread,
Smell the salt of the ocean.
All these things often taken for granted
will always be just dreams of the dolphin.

Believe

Seeing is believing.
 Yet what I see can be very different,
 From what you see.
 Who is right?
 Who is really seeing?
 Who is believable?

Believing is trusting.

Yet you can trust someone completely
And not believe them.
Whom can you believe?
Whom can you trust?
Who is really believable?

Trusting is faith.

Therefore,
Seeing is faith.

Journey to the past

Me
Myself
My life
How can I know me
If I don't know those that came before me?
Tracing lines across counties and countries
Following family lines down twisting paths
I belong to royalty
I belong to peasants
The bright tartans of bold green, and gold
The flowing poetry of our family language
Missing
The rolling prairie landscapes
The crumbling stone castles
Forgotten
The legendary family heroes
And brave deeds in the face of adversity
Lost
Or are they?
I bring pieces of my history forward to the present
With each journey, I take to the past
I remember
I retell
I learn
And in that, I know my past
I understand my present
I challenge my future.

Kids

Have kids they said
It'll be fun they said

Through bleary eyes
And a lack of sleep
You reflect on
Parenting and how
Much you should worry
And when you will stop

That mystery stain on your
Shirt at work – probably puke
The colourful artwork
Expressed onto your
Kitchen table –with a sharpie
The bubbles overflowing
your tub –from your shampoo
 The Lego on the bottom
Of your feet – in the dark.

The Mother's Day gift
Made from clay – and love
The Christmas tradition
That started because you
Couldn't wait for them to open it
The Easter Eggs you weren't
Allowed to throw out
The snuggles from bad dreams

 in the middle of the night.
Through bleary eyes
And a lack of sleep
You ponder
He can vote now
When do I stop worrying
and get some sleep.

Have kids they said
It'll be fun they said

Grammar Police

When working in this language
I struggle to really know
The Oxford comma, yes or no?
This is all so terribly new
But I really do wish I knew.
This is all so confounding
Do I tell them that
They're over there
With their plane?
That seemed plain to see
Even if it's sitting by the sea.
I went by the store
To buy some flowers
But the grocer gave me
Two bags of flour
And that is entirely too many.
I don't know where I'm going
So, I have no idea what to wear
I'm quite sure we look the pair
Climbing trees to pick a pear.
Incorrect is something
I really hate to hear
So, I'm asking everyone here
Is it wrong or is it right?
I can no longer write
This piece I think
If I ever want to find some peace
So, before some calls

The Grammar Police
I need to know
Oxford comma, yes or no?

Daddy's Little Girl

I walked her down the aisle,
All eyes were on the two of us.
She looked so beautiful and delicate,
Like a doll in a china shop.
She ran around the house
Laughing and giggling.
She was the most delightful child,
No one could want more.
I hugged her, kissed her, and left her there.
She stood beside a man,
A stranger in my life
And smiled happily.
She was extremely bright,
The teachers all adored her.
The school years seemed to get shorter,
And all too soon she had graduated.
The strange man lifts her veil
To uncover her shining young face.
He places a ring on her finger
And tells her that he loves her.
Her first words were so exciting,
She soon learned many more.
Her first step was taken with care and my help,
Now she would take those steps on her own.
I don't want to see her go.
I hold her close for memories.
"Daddy," she says. "I love you, dearly,"
and away walked daddy's little girl.

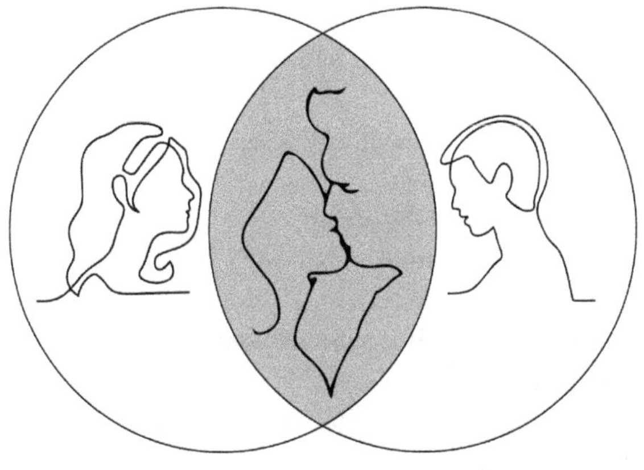

A memory is haunting

I hear her voice.
I see her face, like a ghostly image
Just beyond my sight.
She skirts away, whispering
Long-forgotten words of advice.
I see her smile.
I hear her words, like a distant wind
Rustling the autumn leaves.
She shared my secrets, she wiped away tears
Of broken hearts and shattered dreams.
I hear her laugh.
I see her cry, like raindrops
Running to the lake.
She remains to vent my frustrations,
She remains to exalt in my joy.
Only now, I must be willing to share her,
For she is no longer mine alone.
I see her flowing white gown.
I hear her call my name,
Just like my little sister.

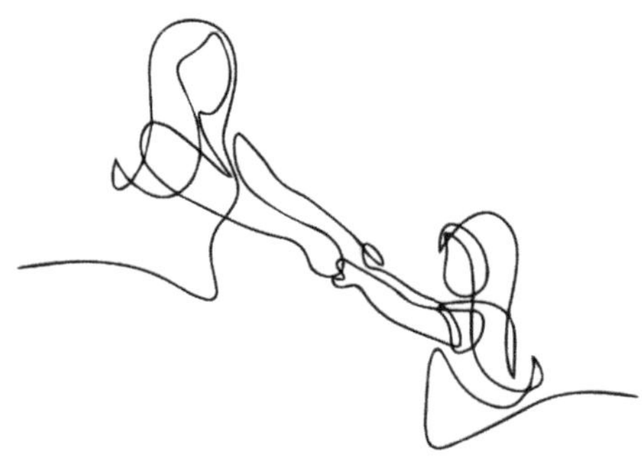

Spectrum

He dances along the spectrum
 Most people never seeing
 The world the way he does
 Thinking our way
 Is the only way

He sees linear patterns
And logical progressions
With his Spock-like observations
Seeing the world through
Connection and not emotion

His brain never slows
Instead working harder
And faster than most
Hearing and seeing everything
All at once

He comprehends more than
People believe
But he doesn't understand
Why no one else can
Dance along the spectrum with him

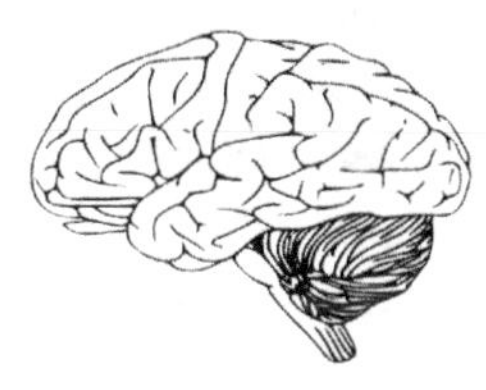

Autumn

With an abundance of apples
Autumn descends upon us.
Between baling in the fields
and back to school the season
is bountiful.
A cornucopia of cider,
Cranberries and corn mazes.
The deciduous trees
Display earthy and enchanting
festive foliage and
gold fields filled with gourds
in time for Halloween.
Taking hay-rides under hunter's moon.
Enjoying Indian summer before
making Jack-o-lanterns.
You pull a jacket on to keep warm
As you linger in the leaves
Of the magnificent maples
And watch the migrating geese.
The night time chill of November is approaching
But the orange of October first brings a
Orchard picking and plethora of pumpkins in
Pies, cookies and breads.
Pull out your favourite quilt
And relax into the season
Of stuffing and sweet potatoes
Turkey and traditions.
While the season is unpredictable,

It is also vibrant and vivid.
A Wonderous and wild,
But it provides a xenial
Place of Zen.

The Waiting Game

I sit here staring at the clock.
Each tick of the second hand
Thunders through my body.
Like a herd of wild horses.

He hasn't texted. Will he?

I feel like a freshman
Worrying about a first date.
If I were any less secure,
I'd break down and weep.

He hasn't texted. Will he?

I have the strength and fragility
Of a butterfly.
I can avoid danger and fly for miles,
But one touch of my wings and I'm grounded.

He hasn't texted. Will he?

Why this flood of emotions?
Why do I really care?
Maybe I could text him,
If my fingers would only push the buttons.

He hasn't texted. Will he?

Ding

Field of Honour

With each visit
The gravestones seem
To slip further and
further back.

The field of honour is kept
Neat and tidy.
The headstones lined up
In silent little rows,
A small reminder of their
Time standing at attention.

The ones at the back
Have faded over the years
Much like our memories
Of their wars.
New ones continually
Place in front.

Poppies adorn each stone
As we continue to remember
But with each visit
The gravestones seem
To slip further and
further back.

Why We Hunt

The autumn breeze
Is cool and damp
But I don't feel it
Right now

I've been out here
for days
searching
finally seeing the one
trying to stay calm
but
I'm too focused
On a finding a good
Sight picture
Are you close enough?
Can you get closer
Without spooking it?

Be Quiet!

I hear a noise
But it's just
my blood pumping
But I hear it
Pulsing in
my ears
In my head
And I feel it

in my arms
In my legs
In my core.

I try to breathe
But my heart rate
Hits one hundred forty-three
Beats per minute
Or maybe seconds
I squeeze the trigger
As I exhale.

This is why we hunt.

Moose Hunt

It had been a long wait
 Scarlet and umber leaves
 Crackling under our feet
 We walked
 Gently picking through
 The decaying undergrowth
 Trying to stay as hushed
 As the woods around us.

The air biting at our cheeks
Exciting racing
Through our veins
My gun felt light on my shoulder
As we start out
It won't stay that way
The longer you push bush
They heavier it gets.

He's anxious
It's not his first moose hunt
But it's not the same as before
His hunting partner isn't here
This season is running out
His seasons are running out
So, he's stuck with me
The moose hunt virgin

The day moves on
The daylight starts to melt

into the glowing tree line
It's a bust
We were skunked
Our heads hung lower
As we made our way back
Out of the muskeg.

He points out the important
Landmarks in the bush
"I got that big buck
Just over there"
"They've been bedding down
Right in here"
I nod trying to absorb
All of this knowledge.

But I don't remember those trees
Are those legs in the field?
Yes, there's your moose
Dad
The adrenaline hurtles in
As he raises his rifle
My first moose hunt is a success
Hopefully, it's not our last.

Printed in the USA
CPSIA information can be obtained
at www.ICGtesting.com
LVHW020415071224
798552LV00003BA/547